Anansi

TWO MINUTES FOR HOLDING

Also by Douglas Burnet Smith

TWO MINUTES FOR HOLDING

Meditations on Love
and Other Infractions

DOUGLAS BURNET SMITH

Anansi

Published in 1995 by
House of Anansi Press Limited
1800 Steeles Avenue West
Concord, Ontario
L4K 2P3
Tel.(416)445-3333
Fax (416)445-5967

Canadian Cataloguing in Publication Data
Smith, Douglas, 1949-
Two minutes for holding
Poems. ISBN 0-88784-567-3
I. Title.
PS8587.,58T86 1995   C811'.54   C95-930325-1
PR9199.3.S66T86 1995

Cover design: General Theory
Printed and bound in Canada

*House of Anansi Press gratefully acknowledges the support of the Canada
Council, the Ontario Ministry of Culture, Tourism, and Recreation, Ontario
Arts Council, and Ontario Publishing Centre in the development of writing
and publishing in Canada.*

Yet I have never found what I write in what I love.

— Paul Éluard

A primary thaw
Set between provinces of snow
The winter night scheming perfect architecture
Eye contact would be
Lethal *begin* you could have said
I already had in the mirror begun
To melt down
Begging myself not to
But your wrists
Carrying the silence
At the beginning of their name held me
Gone I was gone

Looking for a place to be
Free of charm and dictation
Unswayed by the swaying of the charmed
Body in black I will follow to "die"
For your downcast look then a hooked seed
The wrong pages turning in me you bending
Back the corners of new ones
A marked man
Unrecognized though hours later
Imprinted with one touch

How many lives to get here
To martial passion walking to the car
Small waves wrinkling breaths
What fulcrum were we banishing
Who took a pass
At the blue line
Breaths that soon would be
Softer than confidence
A silver unit
Small talk turning over
A huge engine
Before we knew it we were
Conducting ourselves

Yes your wrists their dark native lines
Taking me around them along
An orbit of arms inked
Where else do you have these colourations
What is the probability of
An ankle I can kiss
Let logic take care of itself
Lips said *heart* trembling
Never in a poem

The coast of fear
Approaching the sweet nevertheless
Definitive fingers interlocking
(A quick wrist shot)
A poppy coming in you
This time we're both right
Fear of being left
Out beyond your slender vowel I sail
The cloth of cliché
Regardless of the upper register
And the dark of shuddering hair

So many seconds passed like crimes
Until *yes* you said
Yes we can go there
And my authorship was admitted
I was allowed
Sequence dissolved in wine
Some hinge turned
A single look and I was lost in rain
You knew you would fly toward me
The apple held in your mouth
Swallow uncontained

Like trying to get comprehension to change
Quick longing, a novella, a
Zero to sixty psychosis
I was debris you gathered what sorrow
Undressed its context and laughed
Everything came out of you
All representation, the tender force
We were just going to sleep
Restraint the operative cold star we
Could steer by to stillness
So much for intention one faint
Wrist and ankle all of you
Speaking of it makes a poor ghost
The exact moment of discontinuity "ended"
Everything I wanted my hands spilled

What kind of election was that first one
(A glimpse made monarch)
Tithing wrists the blue arteries the blue
Ink taking me into armed tyranny
The downcast look (I was an easy mark)
First vote cast down mastered
Lips ministering the throat
The government of pulse
No confidence in the speaker
No language for any of it
This is an example
Of swirl, balance
Gone I was gone armed
To the teeth
Marks just below your shoulder

This time we're both
Implants deeper than shadow
A floating ovary an eye
Opening in the dark
Cold with covers pulled off
Suspicion out for a run
The hill of one hip I can run
A blue hand over the water
In your eyes everything sinks
Fate vessels

Currents a body of thought
At dawn twists in my hands
On the way to the car we prayed for anything
To hold on to

"Overtime" received
A number of awards
For its unspeakable fiction
Dim light making the transition
New bodies' horizontal gestalt
Eradicated touch
From the vocabulary failing desire

We paused on the embankment
Night listed under your tongue
Birds floating past
Murky prepositions
Possessives on the futon
I knew I'd been accomplished
I knew I'd been won

Against a backbeat
Habitual versatility of the pulse
Like riding a state of silence or a bicycle,
You wanted verity, an entry
There was that small electric clock
Red eyes hovering over pillows
Those closures so continuous
We opened many branches in new locations

Intention and improvisation, the backbone
We shared sides leaving
Blind as nipples
I love it when
When being gone
A slow honeyed spiral
A face-off circle
A black parted mane

What we *don't* talk about when we
Overlap, the object of self
A sky leaking perfection
One piece of perfect pink broken burning ice
For a long time I couldn't remember
Who were you in another life
Pushing your babies out
I needed to be there having your mouth
Pushing against my neck like the past
A stone falling out of a dream
Into the wine you taste on that part of me
That's gone, pushed
A pushover

Digression flowers
So I can't understand your shudders
Any reference to reality was a smell
The shrug of disorder
As you pulled me down precisely
Pulling my sweater over my head
Because I was a certain age
I was chicken, premature
Pathetic though I could have lasted
Longer than bread rising
Than the need for detail when
It was the gonest thing

The perfect fit
The fit of contortion
Standing or *lying*, a stem bent
Almost to the breaking point
We're nouned
Seek continuity in creases
"The warm social exchange
Makes for a decent release"
Every condition has a sex
Change, it cannot fluster
The new genre of courage

I caught the word-breath hissing
A coffin sliding over ice
Synonymous desires, palm vector
Nothing *meant*
Face to face face to back: enthusiasms
The implications of the word
Eclipse
The moon is gone but still
Thinking of you

A distinct invitation
To trace the mountainous line of hips
Every line an exaggeration
Snow melting away from the glass
There were fissures in it
We patched handicapped angels

At your disposal
I can be myself now I can't
Tell the difference between this that
Slipping out of you wakes me very amusing
Especially being one who isn't possessed
Of what is considered "originality"
In composition
To be composed these days and years
The narrative needs lubrication
So you push me away

A kiss, lip stitches on the forehead
Transcribed by profiles
I lie another way without you paralysed
Hold me, "a beautiful typeset
Quotation," like one of those deals
Detectives put up on walls (on TV)
When they're trying to track down a criminal
This is no crime to imagine
Being old without having known
Passion staring out a window
No one to receive the gaze
An empty parking lot
A car that won't turn over
And over have we got transmission
Trouble with the story here

The segue is dead . . .
Scribbled under an inquisitor's harsh
Light that bears me further away
At the moment of delirium (perfect fit)
But that's another story: photos
Drawings, postcards (Russian), small paintings
What we make of each other
Terrible manuscripts we have saved
Oh, well all is well when you lean down

The background for all this
(The body beaten is the body —
Lost) nothing draws me toward you
A moist lurch
Constructs a world a head wound
Against my face doesn't exactly
Cover it

You mean you can catalogue this
The place of honour
We share noon two hands
Indistinguishable
The synthesized notes of the watery dream
Reproduction out of the question
Intuition is in ambiguities
Thirteen ways of looking at seven kinds
A vase of moments
A fine and private place

If we were to go on
Consulting a mirror lying lengthwise
Out on the same limb
Asking that infamous antimetaphysical
Question about the deepest questions
What nerve
I send through your spine
"An unusual and intelligent first novel"
Which is the foreground which
The rear whose kiosk is this anyway
What is the price of admission —
Hair just over the eyes (looking down)
Hair just over the shoulders (bearing down) —
Sweet moans
And furthermore your hoarse voice
Gallops from one cleft to the next
This is not a description
A body can finally determine

Think of silkworms, thread-shrine
Congealing, a waterfall
Vestments of the nerve palace
"We wore each other
Out," ourselves almost ourselves
Wet paths woven, deranged
Spools whirling in the candlelit workshop
No seconds here (the clock mulls this over)
Merchandise with no imperfections
Paisley diamonds glisten in a palm

We were all for extending our audience
(Thousands doing the wave)
"Seeing these great works together in one volume
Readers will savour a distillation . . . "
Open at any page read backward sideways
A new directions paperback
You rise at five to sit the traffic
Through old rain playing (your breathing)
Off against
What I process
On the screen, rain's
Book booked solid till noon

In long grass, under northern stars
Shivering fumbling
One leg freezing one hand mouth
On fire, a pitiless movement
We get used to (channel selection
The blood trying to find a way out)
Headlights' soft tracks in the dust
The one note you hum endless and southern

Thank you saliva thank you
Hardness and softness
Thank you lips teeth tongue tongued thanks
Nipples and their small fires thank you hair
Thanks a million perfumed secretions
Our Lady of Lubrication merci buckets
The downcast look tattoo on the ankle thank
You clefts scars stretch marks bruises hollows
Thank you wrists eyelid-pulse shadowed thighs
Rigid slack jaw tightening fists opening thank you
Sleep

Lyric theatre studio — your voice armed
"Like wind through trees in heaven"
A celebrated story of love and regret (rush seats)
Passion to problem: red shift
Such a thing as too fast too strong
A word sweeping it all away
Fragments the person
The one with whom one
Talks performs more and more the one
Who cherishes the cherished
Rising up, lightly
Bitten fruit
Being swallowed

Your exact position arms thrown
Back reaching for the pushing for the
Wall centuries of force in that gesture
The mirror giving it all a painful stare

But most of all knowing you would
Announce me conducting silence
With knife and fork in a gauzy restaurant
Knowing you would kiss taste sweat faint
In the wine at the corner of my mouth
Knowing the paisley of this comforter, animacules
Overheating bellies and vision would be
Notes sounding only then, one note
A long moan of snow
Pouring down the mountain

Whoever wants what is not there
No one is clear on this
Perdito Perdito
I'm taller when I kneel
Back to bed, partly you're poised
Promising love in another world
Nothing can save us not even
The risk of the fragment
One side of your face
Roused native to take leave
Of yourself that placed my hands
Everywhere ignorant of geometry

The action has no location
Dissolved into a pronoun so indefinite
Entrance from the right wing of a relative clause
A current in the sheets crackles
Fine hair, too, a triangle
A blank agreement a *bassa danza*
Neither is named simply amazed
At the other's intrepidity, a symptom
It remains to be seen if I am
Representing myself as an ordinary player
Or if I disappear in line seven

Inserting, tactics
Triangulate (the goal between us) desire
Prefer pursuit to capture
The eyeball, some falling
Projectile a voltage discharged
Eyelids important
"I want to say something to you"
The veiling motif begins
If there is a simile, it stays inaccessible
Emended, launched out of icy
Misapprehensions: *We have to talk*
A compound experience a unit of sound
Your throat's
Beautiful climbing

Interval: glance and reach
Teaching me what an edge
Is, defied, deified, dissolved the tongue
And taste
A comic part of me is gone in the first round
Lucid expropriation
"What a loser"
Your coming is a drift of possibilities
A knowledge of nothing in the actual

Is melting a good thing
Don't ask
Ice you remain a solid
Stickiness I have such a longing
For, a perfect economy
A caesura between eyes and mist

This completes my violation
You staged the robbery in a fit
Of *unh unh*
Edges are irrelevant in the epic
Floe of postures as you dream
The warmth out of your lungs caught
In small hesitations, the space
Between the letters in   *l o v e*   lying undetected
In the alphabet

You wrenched the syntax
Of this solitude, produced
In me a new vowel
Lips blowing across
The narrow mouth of a bottle
(The wine long gone long reconstituted)
The resonance of trust
In sign language, a sound
Language (tongue, teeth, palate, lips, nose)
A delighted discomfort
An informed archaic inscription
Between the legs

I'm scrawling this because
That act simply floors me please help me
Up you read anything
You want into this, don't you
You'd construct the whole thing
Differently, user control freak
To replace the actual with
The ideal doesn't (this) have something to do
With transference

So much for oneness so much
For pyramids, the way knowing
Acts in the mind as opposed
To hips or lips
(Think about what that feels like)
Your wonderful hiding place
A vessel where I can look back out
At myself where I can look back out
Not seeing myself
The understudy through a one-way
Mirror, home of the disillusioned virtuoso

The position was not an easy one
But became easier gradually
As we talked about it wrote it
Down a congenital literacy interrupted
By description of the place, the scene —
White futon Navaho comforter
Lemon candlelight or bright
Afternoon (once only the stairs'
Green carpet provided an inclination) —
Strengthened our ligaments so we could stay
Like that for as long as we
Did not need to

I got in a cab for the airport
Looked back up at you windowed
White silk hard nipples
(The downcast gaze) and
I wanted you with me under
Me on top legs pushing me against the back
Of the front seat the driver politely
Ignoring us going through the motions
Of the archetypal pile-up
But you waved and turned away away I went
So long that cornball phrase
It's all in my head though I'm exquisitely sore
Elsewhere

Yes there's a bitterness
To all this how could there not be
Having got what
I wanted

You're floating down from the sky billowing
Red skirt silk blue blouse
Arms stretched behind fingers
Of one hand shifting
The motive of the moon
You bring it to me a vertigo
An opponent whose face keeps
Changing growing more beautiful fragrant
Telling me this in a whisper
Sentence which is merely *his, his*

We mimed the villanelle
Where flowers open
At night close in the sun
Reversing nature reversing
Our field cutting back
Against the grain the kernels
Of your chest burned
Mine

You need to go back
A long way to find ones
So amusingly pained
(A battery of shivers)
Labouring under enforced left-handedness
Surprise
Both the method of the kiss and its
Meaning a lippy dialogue
Dawn coming in all
Grainy and gloomy softening
The moral texture (until it felt convincing
To the touch)
The bed looks salvaged from
Some sunken castle

Contusions, marks of the game, knowledge
Of the centre a cold original
Pleasure deep blue in the hollow
Of the nape opening like an orchid
An iris one vivid example
Quite new every time
"Now then" over and over again
The petal of this suction
Blooming to fade to turn time
Into skin its colourful perversities

It trivializes the site
The metaphor "embedded"
The sight of glory became a deadfall
Merely textual though touch
Has everything to do with it
"That would be a moment of wrenching pain"
(The downcast look, the myth)
Of separation, of leaving
You a sound not heard before
A gasp *put me back take me back*
Into your delicious heat

The position of the particle and its velocity
Impossible to measure without
Alteration, love's alteration finds
Wedged, between us two
Tenses one rather long sigh
Too late (not again) to avoid desire
Your gaze made me
Lose breath when I saw it
Not even the vantage point of the mirror —
Everything reversed — could do any good
Though what *good* is, being composed,
"There is no time when" I am and am
Not some theory of your arms

An instrument that knows
Only the fingering
Of pleasure's distinctions
That, yes, that
What we live in and what lives
In us a perfume stronger
Than memory, a memory of itself
The places on each other
We have travelled and stayed
Dark rushes banks
We can slip into the river
From, dressed undressed
Thinking not thinking

This is shudder
This is whisper
This is the pressure of gratefulness
This is a ready tongue
This is so we can forget old answers
This is moist susceptibility
This is a hip check
This is static announcing our intentions
This is biting, a new art
This is shadow under a cheekbone
This is drawing my hand away
This is you putting it back
This is time out
This is hours in the car along a shore of stacked
       blue-white
This is the curve of one calf
This is being able to say almost what we mean in a
       bankrupt restaurant
This is running out into poor moonlight
This is never being subject

Meanwhile snow
On the firs has made a cold garden
How cold can vision get
When the body storms
Its various parts shake for want of
Skin that is burning to
Its depths frozen in its moving
Toward nothing we can name
Nothing your eyes
Find frightening and welcome
Me deep and well into

And yet there seems to be
No stopping place for this unrefused
Pleasure, ice on a hot stove, no mere
Metaphor we're talking about,
Delicate and steady
Transgression, thought impossible
But proved by the way you
Hold me in delay along the perimeter
Of your entire length (confused)
Waiting for one of us to move or not
Move there seems to be
No difference

Fat light
Of the afternoon covering
Your shoulders, narrow
Coordinates I can locate
The world from, all its interruptions
However beautiful and catchy —
Waxwings trying to hurry
The last snow off a spring branch —
This is the moment washed
Laid out to dry and stiffen the moment
You go missing
Except for shoulders
Charting a perfect progress

A long sleep intermittently you appeared
On various sets
Of stairs and performed
Wonderful acts of kindness
Upon the two-dimensional uncertainties
Of my face and chest

Crucial are the dextrous
The sequence pretentious inversions
Such as this
We move against our own naturalism
What word can I use
Except *phrenzy*
Some red lily bursting

Grey-blue wash and white bodycolour
Over pencil on grey-blue paper —
You sleeping, early spring morning
"I do not know anything in
Studies of this rapid kind more beautiful
Than the rapt expression of your face"
Some kinda chiaroscuro portrait:
Eyebrows drawn fine cross-hatching
In the lives
Of their growth, absolutely pure
Strength in their double arch
The nose straight equally strong
Lips unerringly
Apart, parted, the hair in musical
Curls ordered disordered
A need to get all this right
The blessing of the throat
Tapering does not
Taper the silk that deepens its blue
Tint at your shoulder under all
That is dark grey already called "hair" darkened
In its masses, blurred by the inked
Shadow grafted on to everything by shadow

Moments we lose
Control of the figuration, as parts of us
Recombine or slip
Out of their couplings mirror
Each other as quotients
To see this we need to backtrack
(All pattern as well as all mimesis)
Glistenings piercings stainings burnishings
All enlargement, and all diminution
Of adorning thought

You're crouching
In front of the kid just slapped like a puck and sobbing
The mother flicking ash off a cigarette
Past your face
Into the wind of January
Convenience stores and "shrinking social services"
Nothing to hide we are comfortable being
Comforted by new nakedness
Every star is doubled
Is there nothing random about all this

If it rains
We stay in bed the sky dolphins its clouds
Down just for us we pretend
It needs our attention from the second floor
(The rhythm section)
Both tired of our names
Remembering these roles have been
Reversed: "You're the guy in this relationship"
White nightshirt bunched at the top
Of your thighs a uniform wetness
On the other side of the pane
Flaking paint diamonds
What we are engaged to
The rest of the day will never catch up with

Where drama has to come from
It's ancient
Talking about how you want it done just after
It's done by the time you read
This the scene will be of course over
Or never even begun
Your patience to let speech
Dissolve not rush
Into touch, into lyric heat
Nothing spoken mechanically everything
Done by hand

Austerity of black and white
A vast poem founders
The trip takes longer, evidence
Of violence and greed
Everything faded desiccated like this
Petal's paleness all that's left
Of its blue life on the Spanish Steps
Courting disaster
Through deliberate formal subversion

Cornflowers, kiwi, black
Coffee, newspapers smudging comforts
Of dreamed regularity
And partial seclusion, refusing
Habit any sufficiency a backhanded habit itself
We don't want to be starlings
About this internal life we aren't
Accustomed to nesting

November blue gabardine evenings
As if I were only able to *say*
We were in Avignon or looked
Out over the rooftops of Rome, lemon trees
Forming a bright line on one side
And the proverbial rusty terracotta sunset
On the other deep in the milky
Bath I remember you tired glistening
The shutters sliced light
Perfectly across the sheets
If there were a camera
Angle it would have been
Perspectiveless enormously valuable in
Its devalued emptiness (but there is nothing
Here that could remind you of anyone's movie)
Maybe I was too sensitive to what I had
So to speak done to you
To the edge of your face with the inside
Of my wrist, that is, softly, twice over

The more I remember the more
I invent boulevards drenched
Or dusty tasks accomplished
With an amorous flinch you say
It's a cinch this technicolour ardour
This kite-flying turbulence
An épaulement, a good, tight, fifth position
Grackles have made a friendly
Amendment now we can vote on the motion
Smile when you say that
You've made silent promises
I want to be held on principle
To your mauve sky

Let me never forget o god of the conjured
Memory you leaning way out beyond
The Norton engine challenging the fulcrum
Point between two tires taking
A long curve and
Skimming pavement with the heel of a black boot
The pressure of your knee against
The small
Of my back you dreaming this
(In Stanfields) in loyalty
To our last kiss the one we won't know
Is our last due to
Death or some other singular freezing over

The first grievous injury
Less this imbroglio of verbiage
Getting stronger as you
Fall apart
Accident-tasselled we looked ahead
And saw the "as," the "if"
Well the room was very small was
A box when we weren't
In it, or it in us as the myth
Of irresistibility toward
Looks, bones and features conducted
Its recruitment, including
A grimy moon that doesn't fit here
Except to mediate the grimace
We're trying to bandage by not
Not coming again

We woke up to displaced stars
And worn stones
Between the Baptistery and Giotto's tower
A young German accompanying himself
On tape in front of The Gates of Paradise
"It's a Wild World"
This is such a relief, a frescoe
Under the whitewash of the world
(All appalling alliterations)
Which is why we can read on a wall
Mulceo, dum loquor,
  Varios induta colores —
"I caress as I speak, dressed
  In many colours"—
Without feeling redundant or
Conceited because we're holding
Hands your legs cooling on the sides
Of a tall thin misted glass
In the warm shade of the Duomo near
The end of a century

Undoing buttons is a Neruda canto
Reactionary buttons revolutionary fingers
It isn't summer
Skin that is warmer than anything
We've ever trusted
(Blouse falling to the floor)
Cut to you, earlier, rubbing slow motion perfume on
        the insides
Of your legs now I'm drifting
Away in it I can't stand it balance
Having been far too much of an effort
From the start

Into whose ear blood "pounds"
Or does it frolic all frisky and
Super-happy to be moving and on its
Way out   *you're not listening*
How could I, I'm distracted, I'm floating
Give me back my weight
(The ref makes a bad call)
I want your full weight
The eardrum translating transmitting
Words that are vibrations before
Anything else, at the simplest uniform level
You dress in complete black tenderness

As the snow floats down
On the Quai d'Orsay it swirls up too
Stomp so the pigeons
Can do their iridescent take-off and ellipsis
Earlier in the morning your lips
Moved the same way then there was no time
We had to be out of the room
Because the river can be imagined as the Seine
Even though it shouldn't be this grey
Will I know you
When this bridge no longer looks like
A silver broach what ring
Would you have me wear
To ensure this is happening in another life

Postfeminist lips blowing on hot tea
We were tangled without deliberate need
Of political breast-kissing, pulling hard
On each other's nipples hard
You couldn't see in the mirror
Positioning of a face
A state under siege of hair
The future prepared for without clothes
Sleep was a martialled contentedness
Even now I recall hints for the code
You dreamed in another language, repeatedly
Saying my name blanketing me with it
Like a frost

There must be another word
Besides infraction for this condition
The poem goes blue in the face
Loving compression unanticipated
The blue of your softly given bruise gone yellow
Like an infinitive waiting to happen
The blue of the snow complicating the day
With pastels fans lifting the grey of a fish
Up out of the river to the sky a cycle
Of thawing and freezing
In a tremor of sex, "no longer us" constantly blue
In the passive voice

Holding out
For word from the next room
"Trick," perhaps, will keep us
From dividing ourselves from the event
So that sex would be something unnecessary
And inevitable, inhalation
An entire plot unfolding on the first page
However dangerous faith in language,
A word, it can be megastress
But you say take a pill
And put me in your mouth

Stains of smashed raspberry on the sheet —
One part of light through the prism
In a window closed to misunderstanding
But not to places sucked
Swollen, conspiracy of repetition
(Love is a repetition; some prairie boy's easy axiom)
Language not needed for comparison
Just hands and exhaustion

In the violet light of the tube, cat's-eye
Green of the tuner (no disc), in the thrown
Winnowed shadows of reflected streetlight leaves, it's
          perfectly
Demonstrated that you bend naked
To the quotidian gesture: pulling on
Jeans, slipping prohibitive hooks
Flippantly out of a failed clasp —
Sometimes, before this, conversational with the early light
Sometimes silent as you return from the shower
A little damp and quite warm
Arms no wristwatch yet
No bracelets leaving their silver imprints
Under my shoulder just a steady almost
Anonymous motion that would
Leave anyone else — God forbid — breathless

There was a solstice dividing
Daylight pulp of the orange
"I would like you to hold this deep inside"
Sinus congestion
The sign for "us" late in the season beginning
With white noise, that is, silence of snow
Across the bridge the *Isle* lighting up
Things as they are, welcomed
You handed me
A breathy treatise

Everything thereafter had lost its place
Waiting, in line, or benched, the words tried to stand
In for each other (falsified passports)
I gathered your age was a Tibetan hat
We travel apart always to the same garden
The light moves there over you
A flotation device
A seeing into what had been your arms
Lilac, iris, rose gathered in them
You hit the command for flight
I lost three words that day
Ravished at the flaky door of the Louvre

Now and then, a couple of faces, "seem" and "seemed"
Ours, explaining intimacy
Hours with you voiceless
April never arrived
A female duration loved French poetry
Years later we will find ourselves doubting
Any kind of contact outlawed
On black ice you can lose control
Of the sentence your last chance

Connective tissues
Let nations strike medals in their names
We visited each other's museums
Falling asleep would be cool trust
You showed me yours
Then the music arrived, *Court and Spark*
Under the comforter my exaggeration bowed down
First light through rice-paper blind
Only connect, sure sure

Sweat-salt corroding the backs of watches
Hands leaving warm pools on the body
Microclimates always surprising
Neck prismatically sucked
Please be seated the performance is about to be kissed
Mint-green sage arranged like spokes
On a big white plate, your hand offering
A mouth
A stoppage in play

You smell incensed
Sex on the sleeve of your robe
Will you look at this and tell me what you taste
Write me into cities
You remember and please remember their bells
The tongue of a bell at your throat
Look out over shingles of the capital glittering
Acting casual or causal
Put it in reverse so you can forget
Your studied repose enlarges me
Until I don't fit in the frame

Skylight window with trellised Rambler roses and clematis
Leaded Favrite glass c.1920
We fit into this (postcard) room
Nicely adaptable to the pull
Of illumination from earlier time
We would have had to touch
Through furbelows, waistcoat, stays,
Flushed brows, pendulum chimes
Of alarm of temptation of face and neck
And rose-water belly I'd be resting
One open hand on no matter how closed
The minds of courtship had made
Decisions from, somewhere a long dark way off

Every rib on one side a rumour of the
Other bending right, mirrored
Dark, circles around the eyes or nipples
You coughed all night like a foetus
I wanted to pull out of the dark
The letter that never was
We left in Provence
If you think it's a chain you must have
Kissed reopened me illegally in mist

Huge cotton Tuscan pillows
City of thirteen towers
Perfect view of
Thunder between balustrades
Before I could say never again you
Mathematically eliminated
Whoever invented the Torture Museum
Pleasant little stream rippling by
McDonald's just around the corner

Shoulder-love

The registration deadline has been extended
To the curve of your hip
Crystal flakes speeding up sunlight
There is nothing to turn from
Lower your voice near water
Don't forget the error of my eyes
Would you have looked back
Under a triple threat
What useless tree do you think
You could have learned to conform to

Take me into your
Confidence brilliance
Not necessarily in that order any order
"'I should have been a pair of' silver skates"
You reserved the sun porch
For writing and fucking
Let X represent vagrant time
How *does* the blue water behave
We face each other's warmth
Wondering what haven't we done
To bring on such dizziness

Those red damned eyes of the clock
Intermittently waking exhaled dream
Where children have been playing war
You send me
A sore ear
You move against my definition of stream
Tear at perforation
My twin your shadow glares
The wine into which the moon is tumbling
(The lines on your wrists the circle of things
You call your own)
The usual breakfast of stolen fruit

Delusion an augmented fifth
There is more stick work now
That there are visors
You raised a hand to shade your eyes
I counted on everything
We told identical lies
(Was that possible) in the blue dusk
Of November poorly organized
Clouds towers doves old leaves

"Nothing now left sacred,
In the places where once —
Nothing was profane"
But that was in the future
Still a point of concourse
Yet of a different character
As if we spent our lives
Mainly in pleasure
(Wine, pears, gorgonzola
Chestnut blossom grove by moonlight —
White futon still life)
There must be a penalty for all this
Sitting out the game one of us
Temporarily lusting for silence
Imagining the other vital with another
So that (to rejoin the play petition
Must supplant volition) if I ask you to
Bring down the moon you will

Morning voice
A little huskier
Deeper in my ear small fires
Going out a pyre of woodwinds would
Be too much maybe not
I can't wear you I have a better idea
One you'd like if that cardinal
In the sycamore weren't so distracting
One you'd court
Perhaps if it involved embracing me
As a felon
My nape is bite red come on
Make this a record heist

I should have said "record harvest"
Because it was November
And the decision in your favour
A bamboo branch strewn with wishes
Amorous privacy: blue and white porcelain bowl
With morning glories set against a square
Lacquer tray, "a beautiful assemblage"
Gather in every stupid memory
Every perfectly flushed sky over
(Don't ask me what this means)
What poets used to call the "heart"
Skylarks replaced by Buicks
I don't think I can
Go on

With your pen
Neurological changes
I write
Because it has a selfish smell because
It's the year of the lion I love
Your side of the bed, and story
Dreams (seemingly) without distortions
Conflations, displacements, camouflages,
And latent content, "a series of
Breathtaking, confessional albums" —
Lines full of middle-of-the-night
Distractions parenthetically quoted words
Like like, dread and entrapment
Come up a lot in an endless hallway
Leading, well, nowhere, a clown
The best I can do is laugh, figure
When you'll disappear not how
Don't I got brains

Thanks for the beautiful blue buttons
Fasten me where I've never been
Remember it's one thing to fast
Another to speed
Into the boards head first
Causing paralysis like this
Mattress life, detached from knowing
Movement from the waist down,
From what an ensemble
Piece this has been all along

Dig these confections
The kind that, uh, "come
From inside," a sunset
Persimmon-red magnetic on one cheek
I can't wait to touch barely
Getting through hours not days
Pastures impossibly located by
Public announcements
That each time we taste each other
We must report to the official
Moon the official sunset or storm filtering
Froth-light, yes, it's a big bucolic duty
To admit even knees are creamy

You I could feel you
Dying cell by cell
And we both locked
In on that, sugar everywhere
In us converted
To the blood's higher purpose, on purpose
You did this like a paper
Clip, I've become so
Attached to your emptiness
The sad aesthetics of it all
A bare desk-top memo
Pick me up and read me
I could be worth
Keeping

I can't do this
I was the hood
Over an engine you couldn't find the release
For, a strange
Tapping inside you had to take apart
The whole transmission to figure
Out where the damage was
A few of my horses missing
Save the rest if you can get your hands
Dirty reach right in don't mind the grease
The little rusted filings I've had
Previous owners you can tell
(Don't bother piecing me back together)
Because that conceit has gone way too far

Congratulations on an amazing new name
Wish I could guess
It hinted by scattering maple leaves
The guests have left, the intimacy is over, the rain beats down
In a smiling doorway
You come across
Like art all surface and depth
The bridge by which all distances are
Measured brings us softly
Together is how it should read but
Issues interrupt always
Like making love without making love
With these cauliflower ears
I don't hear too good
Anymore miracles, question mark

Devout isn't the word
Maybe *withdrawal* with
The drier going just to keep the whole
Affair droning along the scent
Of damp clothes a fixture
A ceiling fan pushing the density
Of "us" back down from its ascent
And in the next room another groove
Acid jazz just ahead of
Whatever we hurry to remove
A robe bells around the neck dangerous
Bracelets hurrying
Holy tasks

Anywhere else that
Tree in all its guises
Would be in something
Of a blue period
So a moment becomes particular
In this funny, nearly dark little
Room a gorgeous moth
Flits in and lips
Parted a bit you
Just . . . point
A silent bid
A tree in the abstract
Mannerist elongations

Great slate-grey strait
Shiny *and* opaque
Chiffon oblong charcoal scarfed
Neck with chanelled twilights
May you wash up
No more bodies lost, bloated
Longing for any landscape deaf to
Buoy bells
One for the poems of sad courtship
Two for the "state" lovers govern unadorned
November is your raw eternal colour even
Under ice, the world-veil, and
Three for the sprinkling of salt in my eyes

That first morning pulling
Night remorselessly onward
Worse than religion or a
Turn of season we were
A mist stealing in to dampen contentment
"Songs without words," trickiest of all
Narrative immersions, pleas
Like final wishes
Not to be a double negative
A sound-to-picture transfer facility
Some auteur's classic flooded
With hypnotic obsessions, a neutral pallet, smoky
Pastels of brown, beige, and white
(Skin on skin
An apparition sequence)
Some holiday tropical turquoise fading
To swimming-pool deep cerulean
A two-shot of violence and charity, each naked
Chasing the other until they blur
The drama got glacial
Slating the next take, a choice waiting to be made
Hands thinking
This is more artful than it looks

Tunes float above
The warm olive-lemon dash
A ripe temptation
To float my hand, too, up, and back
"Crosstown Traffic"
Ain't just a raunchy song
Acceleration when we go down
On each other tenderly steady
Shared misère
Makes the body lighter lets it
Wander or wonder blind and self-sufficient
A cake under its icing
Curious, fearful of mouths it somehow knows
Are watering but will never see
To gauge the future the way
A fridge kicks in periodically shuts off
Finding overdrive in the dark
Next to an inviting
Artificially-heated thigh
The end of March and still "below"
Below the level of the blood
The level of black exterior wine interior
Below the feedback level of Jimi's cranked pain
The level of wear and tear on a highway of touchiness
Below sentence dependence
Just humming along untempted
By the mechanics of temptation

Pleasure the eye
Aware that this is all storied by the eye
Discovering dark hair white shoulders
Snowy roof blue sky delicate faint-tinted late winter cloud
The lover-constructed luxury
Of the beloved, black squirrels and jays
Squabble, the foil of pleasure —
A velvety growth of mould on one phrase
A minute black fungus spotting the skin of
A poem about anger and seclusion
Piques the fancy, eh
But the coast when I return is still
As you, sitting, "letting"
Story colour
The trivial blossom

A night names no longer mattered
Ones on spines shelved
Above and around
(Convoy protecting destroyer)
Helped overcome whatever
Doubts were held between
Membranes in the shadow of *Wiesel* and *Lao Tzu* and
Other life-saving vests on
Paper, fighting off history, killing
The penalty, seriality
Lobbing depth charges
The infernal cortège surfaces
In the clear boats of your eyes
Words circulate in them and down
Into kind hands kind because
They know if
Some sound comes
Out of a mouth it's
A shell the deep grooves are (like pages) places
Something else meant to be

Through the act of acting back
Into the act
"I've been here before"
Sprawling dreamily across sheets
Of paper, that is
A tongue licking an ear
Reminds us of first
Snow first fruit, never being more
Loved, more overdetermined by
Taste — fingers lips ears and, you know,
Wherever else holds personal pre-eminence
Of a moment impossibly
Stretched out into a project, a dress
Rehearsal in which face down mouth gaping
Some small wind skates up one side of the body
Becoming the penalized world
It may be

Acknowledgements

I wish to acknowledge my indebtedness to the
following people for helping to make this book
possible: Marie Gillies, David Homel, Angela Rebeiro,
Micheline Rochette, Randal Ware.

Special thanks to Don McKay for meticulous editing.

The Paul Éluard quotation on page *vii* is from *99 Poems
in Translation*, eds. Harold Pinter, Anthony Astbury,
Geoffrey Godbert (Grove Press, 1994). Translation of the
line from Éluard's "The Invention" by Samuel Beckett.